T0096566

Thoughts on
ACHIEVEMENT

THE FORBES LEADERSHIP LIBRARY

Thoughts on ACHIEVEMENT

TRIUMPH BOOKS
CHICAGO

This edition is published by Triumph Books, Chicago,
by arrangement with Forbes Inc.

Library of Congress Cataloging-in-Publication Data
Thoughts on Achievement.
        p.   cm. — (The Forbes Leadership Library)
    Copyrighted by Forbes Inc.
    Includes index.
    ISBN 1-57243-278-0 (hardcover)
    1. Success—Quotations, maxims, etc. I. Forbes Inc   II. Title :
Achievement.   III. Series.
PN6084.S78T45   1998
646.7—DC21   97-52276
                                                       CIP

This book is available in quantity at special discounts for your group or
organization. For more information, contact:

TRIUMPH BOOKS
644 South Clark Street
Chicago, Illinois 60605
(312) 939-3330 FAX (312) 663-3557

Book design by Graffolio.
Cover design © 1998 by Triumph Books.
Illustrations from the Dover Pictorial Archive Series,
used with permission.
Some of the properties in the photograph on the front cover
courtesy of Marshall Field's Corporate Gifts and Incentives.

Printed in the United States of America.

Contents

INTRODUCTION

The moving motive in establishing FORBES Magazine, in 1917, was ardent desire to promulgate humaneness in business, then woefully lacking. . . .

Every issue of FORBES, since its inception, has appeared under the masthead: "With all thy getting, get understanding."

Not only so, but we have devoted, all through the years, a full page to "Thoughts on the Business of Life," reflections by ancient and modern sages calculated to inspire a philosophic mode of life, broad sympathies, charity towards all. . . .

I have faith that the time will eventually come when employees and employers, as well as all mankind, will realize that they serve themselves best when they serve others most.

B. C. Forbes

ACCOMPLISHMENT

A little and a little, collected together,
become a great deal;
the heap in the barn consists of single grains,
and drop and drop make the inundation.

SAADI

———

Ability wins
the true esteem of the true men;
luck that of the people.

FRANÇOIS LA ROCHEFOUCAULD

———

Human freedom
is an achievement by man,
and, as it was gained
by vigilance and struggle,
it can be lost
by indifference and supineness.

HARRY BYRD

Have a time and place for everything,
and do everything
in its time and place,
and you will not only accomplish more,
but have far more leisure
than those who are always hurrying,
as if vainly attempting
to overtake time that had been lost.

TRYON EDWARDS

I don't want to achieve immortality
through my work.
I want to achieve it
through not dying.

WOODY ALLEN

In the practical
as in the theoretic life,
the man whose acquisitions stick
is the man who is always
achieving and advancing,
whilst his neighbors,
spending most of their time
in relearning what they once knew
but have forgotten,
simply hold their own.

WILLIAM JAMES

Excellence,
in any department,
can now be attained
only by the labor of a lifetime.
It is not purchased at a lesser price.

SAMUEL JOHNSON

The day is not far distant
when the man who dies
leaving behind him
millions of available wealth,
which was free for him to administer during life,
will pass away "unwept, unhonored, and unsung,"
no matter to what uses
he leaves the dross
which he cannot take with him.

ANDREW CARNEGIE

He who considers too much
will perform little.

JOHANN SCHILLER

The great felicity of life
is to be without perturbations.

SENECA

He who has health
has hope,
and he who has hope
has everything.

ARAB PROVERB

Knowledge and courage
take turns at greatness.

BALTASAR GRACIAN

You can't build a reputation
on what you are going to do.

HENRY FORD

Great nations
write their autobiography
in three manuscripts—
the book of their deeds,
the book of their words,
and the book of their art.

JOHN RUSKIN

The influence of each human being
on others in this life
is a kind of immortality.

JOHN QUINCY ADAMS

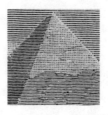

Man only plays
when in the full meaning of the word
he is a man,
and he is only completely a man
when he plays.

FRIEDRICH VON SCHILLER

ADVERSITY

It is not until
we have passed through the furnace
that we are made to know
how much dross there is
in our composition.

CHARLES CALEB COLTON

No one would have crossed the ocean
if he could have gotten off the ship
in the storm.

CHARLES KETTERING

The real test
in golf and in life
is not in keeping out of the rough,
but in getting out
after we are in.

JOHN MOORE

Stones and sticks
are thrown only
at fruit-bearing trees.

SAADI

It is defeat
that turns bone to flint,
and gristle to muscle,
and makes a man invincible,
and forms those heroic natures
that are now in ascendancy
in the world.
Do not, then,
be afraid of defeat.
You are never so near to victory
as when defeated
in a good cause.

HENRY WARD BEECHER

The greatest difficulties
lie where we are not looking for them.

JOHANN WOLFGANG VON GOETHE

Misfortune
does not always wait on vice,
nor is success
the constant guest of virtue.

WILLIAM HAVARD

Real difficulties
can be overcome;
it is only the imaginary ones
that are unconquerable.

THEODORE N. VAIL

He that can't endure the bad,
Will not live to see the good.

YIDDISH PROVERB

There is no excellency
without difficulty.

OVID

What was hard to bear
is sweet to remember.

PORTUGESE PROVERB

In order to succeed,
at times you have to make
something from nothing.

RUTH MICKLEBY-LAND

The great pleasure in life
is doing what people say
you cannot do.

WALTER BAGEHOT

AMBITION

Every man
stamps his value on himself.
The price we challenge for ourselves
is given us by others.
Man is made great or little
by his own will.

JOHANN SCHILLER

The firefly only shines
when on the wing;
so it is with the mind;
when we rest we darken.

PHILIP JAMES BAILEY

As plants take hold,
not for the sake of staying,
but only that they may climb higher,
so it is with men.
By every part of our nature
we clasp things above us,
one after another,
not for the sake of remaining
where we take hold,
but that we may go higher.

HENRY WARD BEECHER

The mightiest works
have been accomplished
by men who have kept their ability
to dream great dreams.

WALTER BOWIE

Whatever course
you have chosen for yourself,
it will not be a chore
but an adventure
if you bring to it a sense
of the glory of striving—
if your sights are set
far above the merely secure
and mediocre.

DAVID SARNOF

Striving for excellence
motivates you;
striving for perfection
is demoralizing.

HARRIET BRAIKER

What you are
must always displease you,
if you would attain to that
which you are not.

ST. AUGUSTINE

We don't know
what we want,
but we are ready to bite somebody
to get it.

WILL ROGERS

Determine never to be idle.
No person will have occasion
to complain of the want of time
who never loses any.
It is wonderful
how much may be done
if we are always doing.

THOMAS JEFFERSON

It is a great deed
to leave nothing for tomorrow.

BALTASAR GRACIÁN

All men dream,
but unequally.
Those that dream at night
in the dusty recesses of their minds
awake the next day
to find that their dreams
were just vanity.
But those who dream
during the day
with their eyes wide open
are dangerous men;
they act out their dreams
to make them reality.

T. E. LAWRENCE

Everyone expects to go further
than his father went;
everyone expects to be better
than he was born
and every generation
has one big impulse in its heart—
to exceed all the other generations
of the past
in all the things that make life worth living.

WILLIAM ALLEN WHITE

CHARACTER

It is not a question
of how much a man knows,
but what use he makes
of what he knows;
not a question
of what he has acquired,
and how he has been trained,
but of what he is,
and what he can do.

JOSIAH G. HOLLAND

Ill fares the land
To hastening ills a prey
When wealth accumulates
But men decay.

OLIVER GOLDSMITH

One's real worth
is never a quantifiable thing.

MALCOLM FORBES

———※———

The man who follows the crowd
will never be followed
by a crowd.

RICHARD DONNELL

———※———

No man can tell
whether he is rich or poor
by turning in his ledger.
It is the heart
that makes a man rich.
He is rich according to what he is,
not according to what he has.

HENRY WARD BEECHER

Make yourself an honest man,
and then you may be sure
there is one less rascal
in the world.

THOMAS CARLYLE

Courage is resistance to fear,
mastery of fear—
not absence of fear.
Except a creature be part coward,
it is not a compliment
to say it is brave;
it is merely a loose misapplication
of the word.

MARK TWAIN

Life only demands of you
the strength you possess.
Only one feat is possible—
not to have run away.

DAG HAMMARSKJÖLD

Courage is not simply
one of the virtues,
but the form of every virtue
at the testing point.

C. S. LEWIS

More people
would learn from their mistakes
if they weren't so busy
denying that they made them.

ANONYMOUS

The highest reward
for a person's toil
is not what he gets for it,
but what he becomes by it.

JOHN RUSKIN

———

We the people
give our nation its character—
and character flaws.

CULLEN HIGHTOWER

———

Life is like a grindstone:
Whether it grinds you down
or polishes you up
depends on what you're made of.

ANONYMOUS

CONFIDENCE

What we think of ourselves
makes a difference in our lives,
and belief in immortality
gives us the highest values of ourselves.
When we so believe,
we achieve proportions
greater than mere matter.

JESSE WILLIAM STITT

Self-distrust is the cause
of most of our failures.
In the assurance of strength,
there is strength,
and they are the weakest,
however strong,
who have no faith in themselves
or their own powers.

CHRISTIAN BOVEE

All the strength and force of man
comes from his faith
in things unseen.
He who believes is strong;
he who doubts is weak.
Strong convictions
precede great actions.

JAMES FREEMAN CLARK

Whoever will be free
must make himself free.
Freedom is no fairy gift
to fall into a man's lap.
What is freedom?
To have the will to be responsible
for one's self.

MAX STIRNER

Nothing is impossible;
there are ways that lead to everything,
and if we had sufficient will
we should always have sufficient means.
It is often merely for an excuse
that we say things are impossible.

FRANÇOIS LA ROCHEFOUCAULD

A true man never frets
about his place in the world,
but just slides into it
by the gravitation of his nature,
and swings there as easily as a star.

EDWIN CHAPIN

To be at peace with self,
to find company and nourishment in self—
this would be the test
of the free and productive psyche.

MARYA MANNES

What recommends commerce to me
is its enterprise and bravery.
It does not clasp its hands
and pray to Jupiter.

HENRY DAVID THOREAU

Lack of will power
has caused more failure
than lack of intelligence or ability.

FLOWER NEWHOUSE

They are able
because they think
they are able.

VIRGIL

The person
who can laugh with life
has developed deep roots
with confidence and faith—
faith in oneself,
in people and in the world,
as contrasted to negative ideas
with distrust and discouragement.

DEMOCRITUS

The world turns aside
to let any man pass
who knows whither he is going.

DAVID S. JORDAN

———

Don't be afraid
to take a big step
if one is indicated.
You can't cross a chasm
in two small jumps.

DAVID LLOYD GEORGE

———

The man who believes
he can do it
is probably right,
and so is the man who believes
he can't.

LAWRENCE J. PETER

One only gets
to the top rung on the ladder
by steadily climbing up
one at a time,
and suddenly all sorts of powers,
all sorts of abilities
which you thought
never belonged to you—
suddenly become
within your own possibility
and you think,
"Well, I'll have a go, too."

MARGARET THATCHER

EFFORT

It is our individual performances,
no matter how humble
our place in life may be,
that will in the long run
determine how well ordered
the world may become.

PAUL C. PACKER

When our efforts are,
or not, favored in life,
let us be able to say,
when we come near
to the great goal,
"I have done what I could."

LOUIS PASTEUR

Some men give up their designs
when they have almost reached the goal;
while others, on the contrary,
obtain a victory by exerting,
at the last moment,
more vigorous efforts than before.

POLYBIUS

Perfectionism
is a dangerous state of mind
in an imperfect world.
The best way
is to forget doubts
and set about the task in hand.
If you are doing your best,
you will not have time
to worry about failure.

ROBERT HILLYER

If you want to earn more—
learn more.
If you want to get more
out of the world
you must put more
into the world.
For, after all,
men will get no more
out of life
than that they put into it.

WILLIAM BOETCKER

Nothing is difficult;
it is only we who are indolent.

BENJAMIN HAYDON

———◆———

Keep on going
and the chances are
that you will stumble on something,
perhaps when you are least
expecting it.
I have never heard of anyone
stumbling on something
sitting down.

CHARLES KETTERING

———◆———

You don't get hits
by trying hard.
You try easy.

GEORGE BRETT

Always seek
to excel yourself.
Put yourself in competition
with yourself every day.
Each morning
look back upon your work
of yesterday
and then try to beat it.

CHARLES SHELDON

Trying
is the touchstone
to accomplishment.

PAUL VON RINGELHEIM

I never worry about action,
but only about inaction.

WINSTON CHURCHILL

Immortality is not a gift,
immortality is an achievement;
and only those that strive mightily
shall possess it.

EDGAR LEE MASTERS

Venture nothing
and life is less
than it should be.

MALCOLM FORBES

There is an old saying,
"The harder you try
the luckier you get."
I kind of like that definition of luck.

GERALD FORD

He who would do some great things
in this short life
must apply himself to work
with such a concentration of force as,
to idle spectators who live
only to amuse themselves,
looks like insanity.

FRANCIS PARKMAN

———

Quality is never an accident;
it is always the result of intelligent efforts.

JOHN RUSKIN

———

Man must sit in chair
with mouth open for very long time
before roast duck fly in.

CHINESE PROVERB

EXPERIENCE

Man really knows nothing
save what he has learned
by his own experience.

CHRISTOPHER M. WIELAND

———◆———

Money is like sea-water:
The more we drink
the thirstier we become;
and the same is true of fame.

ARTHUR SCHOPENHAUER

———◆———

For most men
life is a search
for a proper manila envelope
in which to get themselves filed.

CLIFTON FADIMAN

A race preserves its vigor
so long as it harbors a real contrast
between what has been
and what may be;
and so long as it is nerved
by the vigor to adventure
beyond the safeties of the past.
Without adventure civilization
is in full decay.

ALFRED NORTH WHITEHEAD

———•———

There is nothing
that you can have when you are old
that can replace being young
and having nothing.

MARY WALLACE SMITH

Some luck lies in not getting
what you thought you wanted
but getting what you have,
which once you have it
you may be smart enough
to see is what you would have wanted
had you known.

GARRISON KEILLOR

The greatest mistake
is to imagine
that we never err.

THOMAS CARLYLE

Is there anything in life
so disenchanting
as achievement?

ROBERT LOUIS STEVENSON

If by the time we are 60
we haven't learned
what a knot of paradox
and contradiction life is,
and how exquisitely
the good and bad are mingled
in every action we take,
and what a compromising hostess
Our Lady of Truth is,
we haven't grown old
to much purpose.

JOHN COWPER POWYS

A winner
must first know
what losing's like.

MALCOLM FORBES

Granting our wish
is one of Fate's saddest jokes.

JAMES RUSSELL LOWELL

I have always had a dread
of becoming a passenger
in life.

DENMARK'S QUEEN MARGRETE II

I've learned
that if you laugh
and drink soda pop
at the same time,
it will come out your nose.

7-YEAR-OLD'S DISCOVERY

To live
is like to love—
all reason is against it,
and all healthy instinct is for it.

SAMUEL BUTLER

The secret of what life's all about
Was answered by the sages:
Life's about one day at a time
No matter what your age is.

ROBERT HALF

In the business world,
everyone is paid in two coins:
cash and experience.
Take the experience first;
the cash will come later.

HAROLD GREENE

FULFILLMENT

The meaning, the value,
the truth of life
can be learned only
by an actual performance of its duties,
and truth can be learned
and the soul saved
in no other way.

THEODORE MUNGER

The charm of a deed
is its doing;
the charm of a life
is its living;
the soul of the thing
is the thought.

EUGENE FITCH WARE

There is little peace
or comfort in life
if we are always anxious
as to future events.
He that worries himself
with the dread of possible contingencies
will never be at rest.

SAMUEL JOHNSON

Be ashamed to die
until you have won some victory
for humanity.

HORACE MANN

The great business of life
is to be, to do,
to do without,
and to depart.

JOHN MORLEY

———◆———

Happy is the man
who can endure the highest
and lowest fortune.
He who has endured such vicissitudes
with equanimity
has deprived misfortune
of its power.

SENECA

Loving someone
means helping them
to be more themselves,
which can be different
from being what you'd like them to be,
although often they turn out the same.

MERLE SHAIN

The great law of culture:
Let each become
all that he was created
capable of being.

THOMAS CARLYLE

Perhaps love
is the process of my leading you
gently back to yourself.

ANTOINE DE SAINT-EXUPERY

How shall the soul of a man
be larger than the life
he has lived?

EDGAR LEE MASTERS

—————

What is the use
of acquiring one's heart's desire
if one cannot handle and gloat over it,
show it to one's friends
and gather an anthology
of envy and admiration?

DOROTHY SAYERS

—————

What I still ask for daily—
for life as long as I have work to do,
and work as long as I have life.

REYNOLDS PRICE

If I can stop one heart from breaking
I shall not live in vain
If I can ease one life from aching, or cool one pain,
Or help one fainting robin into his nest again,
I shall not live in vain.

EMILY DICKINSON

⸻

The only joy in the world
is to begin.

CESARE PAVESE

⸻

There are two things
to aim at in life:
first, to get what you want;
and after that, to enjoy it.
Only the wisest of mankind
achieve the second.

LOGAN PEARSALL SMITH

We can secure
other people's approval
if we do right and try hard;
but our own is worth a hundred of it,
and no way has been found
out of securing that.

MARK TWAIN

GOODNESS

Life is made up,
not of great sacrifices or duties,
but of little things
in which smiles and kindness,
and small obligations
given habitually,
are what preserve the heart
and secure comfort.

HUMPHREY DAVY

Unless we give part of ourselves away,
unless we can live with other people
and understand them and help them,
we are missing the most essential part
of our human lives.

HAROLD TAYLOR

The way not to lead
a monotonous life
is to live for others.

FULTON J. SHEEN

Unselfish and noble actions
are the most radiant pages
in the biography of souls.

DAVID THOMAS

No man can make good
during working hours
who does the wrong thing
outside of working hours.

WILLIAM BOETCKER

We make a living
by what we get,
we make a life
by what we give.

WINSTON CHURCHILL

At the end,
the acquisition of wealth
is ignoble in the extreme.
I assume that you save
and long for wealth
only as a means of enabling you
the better to do some good
in your day and generation.

ANDREW CARNEGIE

One thing I know;
the only ones among you
who will be really happy
are those who will have sought and found
how to serve.

ALBERT SCHWEITZER

In the arena of human life
the honors and rewards
fall to those who show their good qualities
in action.

ARISTOTLE

The greatest pleasure I know
is to do a good action by stealth,
and to have it found out by accident.

CHARLES LAMB

When I do good,
I feel good.
When I do bad,
I feel bad.
And that's my religion.

ABRAHAM LINCOLN

What is moral
is what you feel good after
and what is immoral
is what you feel bad after.

ERNEST HEMINGWAY

HAPPINESS

Happiness is an action,
and every power is intended for action;
human happiness, therefore,
can only be complete
as all the powers
have their full and legitimate play.

DAVID THOMAS

If one only wished to be happy,
this could be easily accomplished;
but we wish to be happier
than other people,
and this is always difficult,
for we believe others
to be happier than they are.

CHARLES DE MONTESQUIEU

There is a wonderful
mythical law of nature
that the three things we crave most in life—
happiness, freedom, and peace of mind—
are always attained
by giving them to someone else.

PEYTON CONWAY MARCH

Let all your views in life
be directed to a solid,
however moderate,
independence;
without it
no man can be happy,
nor even honest.

JUNIUS

The most infectiously joyous men and women
are those who forget themselves
in thinking about others
and serving others.
Happiness comes
not by deliberately courting
and wooing it
but by giving oneself
in self-effacing surrender
to great values.

ROBERT MCCRACKEN

What leads to unhappiness
is making pleasure
the chief aim.

WILLIAM SHENSTONE

The art of living
does not consist
in preserving and clinging
to a particular mood of happiness,
but in allowing happiness
to change its form
without being disappointed
by the change,
for happiness,
like a child,
must be allowed to grow up.

CHARLES MORGAN

All happiness depends
on a leisurely breakfast.

JOHN GUNTHER

Half the world
is on the wrong scent
in the pursuit of happiness.
They think it consists
in having and getting,
and in being served by others.
On the contrary,
it consists in giving,
and in serving others.

HENRY DRUMMOND

True enjoyment
comes from activity of the mind
and exercise of the body;
the two are united.

ALEXANDER VON HUMBOLDT

Happiness
is the overcoming
of not unknown obstacles
toward a known goal.

L. RON HUBBARD

My life has no purpose,
no direction,
no meaning,
and yet I'm happy.
I can't figure it out.
What am I doing right?

CHARLES M. SCHULZ

Real happiness is cheap enough,
yet how dearly we pay
for its counterfeit.

HOSEA BALLOU

The goods of Fortune,
even such as they really are,
still need taste to enjoy them.
It is the enjoying,
not the possessing,
that makes us happy.

MICHELANGELO BUONARROTI

I have no money,
no resources,
no hopes.
I am the happiest man alive.

HENRY MILLER

—◆—

I would rather be able
to appreciate things
I cannot have
than to have things
I am not able to appreciate.

ELBERT HUBBARD

—◆—

Enjoyment is not a goal,
it is a feeling
that accompanies important
ongoing activity.

PAUL GOODMAN

Pleasure is Nature's test,
her sign of approval.
When man is happy,
he is in harmony with himself
and with his environment.

OSCAR WILDE

PERSEVERANCE

The greatest results in life
are usually attained
by simple means
and the exercise of ordinary qualities.
These may for the most part
be summed up in these two—
commonsense and perseverance.

OWEN FELTHAM

Your fears can be overcome
if you deal with them properly.
Emotions come wholly from within,
and have only the strength
we allow them.

JOHN WILSON

On the whole,
it is patience
which makes the final difference
between those who succeed
or fail in all things.
All the greatest people
have it in an infinite degree,
and among the less,
the patient weak ones
always conquer the impatient strong.

JOHN RUSKIN

Do not keep away
from the measure
which has no limit,
or from the task
which has no end.

RABBI TARPHON

Big shots
are only little shots
who keep shooting.

CHRISTOPHER MORLEY

Remember,
diamonds are only lumps of coal
that stuck to their jobs.

B. C. FORBES

Great Works
are performed
not by strength
but by perseverance.

SAMUEL JOHNSON

Perseverance
is more prevailing than violence;
and many things
which cannot be overcome
when they are together,
yield themselves up
when taken little by little.

PLUTARCH

Making mistakes is human.
Repeating 'em is too.

MALCOLM FORBES

I have begun several things
many times,
and I have often succeeded
at last.
I will sit down,
but the time will come
when you will hear me.

BENJAMIN DISRAELI

By perseverance
the snail reached
the Ark.

CHARLES SPURGEON

Older generations
are living proof
that younger generations
can survive their lunacy.

CULLEN HIGHTOWER

Without perseverance
talent is a barren bed.

WELSH PROVERB

It is not necessary to hope
in order to act,
nor to succeed
in order to persevere.

WILLIAM OF ORANGE

In the realm of ideas,
everything depends on enthusiasm;
in the real world,
all rests on perseverance.

JOHANN WOLFGANG VON GOETHE

Persistence
is what makes the impossible possible,
the possible likely,
and the likely definite.

ROBERT HALF

A fellow doesn't last long
on what he has done.
He has to keep on delivering.

CARL HUBBELL

PROGRESS

We never reach our ideals,
whether of mental or moral improvement,
but the thought of them
shows us our deficiencies,
and spurs us on
to higher and better things.

TRYON EDWARDS

The world is made better
by every man improving
his own conduct;
and no reform is accomplished
wholesale.

WILLIAM ALLEN WHITE

All progress is based upon
the universal innate desire
on the part of every organism
to live beyond its income.

SAMUEL BUTLER

Our business in life
is not to get ahead of others
but to get ahead of ourselves—
to break our own records,
to outstrip our yesterdays
by our today,
to do our work with more force
than ever before.

STEWART B. JOHNSON

Every art and every inquiry,
as well as every practical pursuit,
seems to aim at some good,
whereby it has been well said
that the good is that
at which all things aim.

ARISTOTLE

Unless we can and do
constantly seek and find ways and means
to do a better job;
unless we accept the challenge
of the changing times;
we have no right to survive
and we shall not survive.

CHESTER FISCHER

Nothing in progression
can rest on its original plan.
We might as well think
of rocking a grown man
in the cradle of an infant.

EDMUND BURKE

So great has been the endurance,
so incredible the achievement,
that, as long as the sun
keeps a set course in heaven,
it would be foolish to despair
of the human race.

ERNEST WOODWARD

Progress
is always the product of fresh thinking,
and much of it thinking
which to practical men
bears the semblance of dreaming.

ROBERT GORDON SPROUT

Very much
of what we call the progress of today
consists in getting rid of false ideas,
false conceptions of things,
and in taking a point of view
that enables us to see the principles,
ideas, and things in right relation
to each other.

WILLIAM HOARD

All genuine progress
results from finding new facts.

JOHN GARDNER

———◆———

After our ages-long journey
from savagery to civility,
let's hope we haven't bought
a round-trip ticket.

CULLEN HIGHTOWER

———◆———

The moving van
is a symbol
of more than our restlessness,
it is the most conclusive evidence possible
of our progress.

LOUIS KRONENBERGER

The simplest schoolboy
is now familiar with truths
for which Archimedes
would have sacrificed his life.

ERNEST RENAN

When you arrive at your future,
will you blame your past?

ROBERT HALF

Two things
we ought to learn from history:
one, that we are not in ourselves superior
to our fathers;
another, that we are shamefully
and monstrously inferior to them,
if we do not advance beyond them.

THOMAS ARNOLD

People in the U.S.
used to think
that if girls were good at sports
their sexuality would be affected.
Being feminine
meant being a cheerleader,
not an athlete.
The image of women
is changing now.
You don't have to be pretty
for people to come and see you play.

MARTINA NAVRATILOVA

———

The most fatal illusion
is the settled point of view.
Life is growth and motion;
a fixed point of view
kills anybody who has one.

BROOKS ATKINSON

A new scientific truth
does not triumph
by convincing its opponents,
but rather because its opponents die,
and a new generation grows up
that is familiar with it.

MAX PLANCK

Amongst democratic nations,
each generation
is a new people.

ALEXIS DE TOCQUEVILLE

RESPONSIBILITY

Have I done anything for society?
I have then done more for myself.
Let that question and truth
be always present to thy mind,
and work without cessation.

WILLIAM SIMMS

If the world is cold,
make it your business
to build fires.

HORACE TRAUBEL

Solvency
is entirely a matter of temperament
and not of income.

LOGAN PEARSALL SMITH

To help the young soul,
to add energy, inspire hope,
and blow the coals into a useful flame;
to redeem defeat
by new thought and firm action,
this, though not easy,
is the work of divine men.

RALPH WALDO EMERSON

Consider what heavy responsibility
lies upon you in your youth,
to determine, among realities,
by what you will be delighted,
and, among imaginations,
by whose you will be led.

JOHN RUSKIN

If it is sensible
for the child to make an effort
to learn how to be an adult,
then it is essential
for the adult to learn
how to be aged.

EDWARD STIEGLITZ

What is virtue?
It is to hold yourself
to your fullest development
as a person
and as a responsible member
of the human community.

ARTHUR DOBRIN

Get all you can,
without hurting your soul,
your body, or your neighbor.
Save all you can,
cutting off every needless expense.
Give all you can.

JOHN WESLEY

If you want to hear
about the power and glory of wealth,
ask a man who's seeking it.
But if you want to learn
of wealth's burdens and difficulties,
ask a man
who's been wealthy a long time.

STANLEY GOLDSTEIN

I am only one;
but I am still one.
I cannot do everything,
but still I can do something.
I will not refuse to do the something
I can do.

HELEN KELLER

Freedom costs you
a great deal.

LILLIAN HELLMAN

REWARD

There is nothing too little
for so little a creature as man.
It is by studying little things
that we attain great knowledge
of having as little misery
and as much happiness as possible.

SAMUEL JOHNSON

The world belongs to those
who think and act with it,
who keep a finger
on its pulse.

WILLIAM RALPH INGE

Health is the vital principle
of bliss.

JAMES THOMSON

No profit grows
where is no pleasure taken;
in brief, sir,
study what you most affect.

WILLIAM SHAKESPEARE

In general,
it is not very difficult
for little minds
to attain splendid situations.
It is much more difficult
for great minds
to attain the place
to which their merit
fully entitles them.

BARON VON GRIMM

A good man
doubles the length of his existence;
to have lived so as to look back
with pleasure on our past life
is to live twice.

MARTIAL

The supreme happiness of life
is the conviction of being loved
for yourself,
or more correctly, being loved
in spite of yourself.

VICTOR HUGO

Health
is better
than wealth.

ENGLISH PROVERB

I keep my friends
as misers do their treasure,
because, of all things
granted us by wisdom,
none is greater or better
than friendship.

PIETRO ARETINO

Even Noah
got no salary
for the first six months—
partly on account of the weather
and partly because
he was learning navigation.

MARK TWAIN

Time cannot be influenced
by mankind.
It gives each of us a beginning,
and an end.
And this makes us question the significance
of what comes between.
But if you can create something
time cannot erode,
something which ignores
the eccentricities
of particular eras or moments,
something truly timeless,
this is a significant victory.

FERDINAND PORSCHE

A true friend
is the greatest of all blessings,
and that which we take
the least care of all
to acquire.

FRANÇOIS LA ROCHEFOUCAULD

Health is a precious thing,
and the only one, in truth,
meriting that a man
should lay out not only his time,
sweat, labor and goods,
but also life itself to obtain it.

MICHEL DE MONTAIGNE

The communicating of a man's self
to his friend
works two contrary effects;
for it redoubleth joys,
and cutteth griefs in half.

FRANCIS BACON

SUCCESS

Put all good eggs
in one basket
and then watch that basket.

ANDREW CARNEGIE

The art of dealing with people
is the foremost secret
of successful men.
A man's success
in handling people
is the very yardstick
by which the outcome
of his whole life's work
is measured.

PAUL C. PACKER

It is with life as with a play—
it matters not how long
the action is spun out,
but how good the acting is.

SENECA

The feeling of having done a job well
is rewarding;
the feeling of having done it perfectly
is fatal.

DONLEY FEDDERSON

The balance
between pride in past achievements
and consciousness of present shortcomings
is difficult to strike.

JOHN O'REN

Men are often capable
of greater things
than they perform.
They are sent into the world
with bills of credit,
and seldom draw
their full extent.

HORACE WALPOLE

Nature
has gave men two ends—
one to sit on
and one to think with.
Ever since then
man's success or failure
has been dependent
on the one he used most.

GEORGE KIRKPATRICK

We succeed in enterprises
which demand the positive qualities
we possess,
but we excel in those
which can also make use
of our defects.

ALEXIS DE TOCQUEVILLE

I have found
that it is much easier
to make a success in life
than it is to make a success
of one's life.

G. W. FOLLIN

Success:
A process of becoming
who you already are.

FRANK POTTS

Success is simple.
Do what's right, the right way,
at the right time.

ARNOLD GLASOW

A man doesn't need brilliance
or genius;
all he needs is energy.

ALBERT M. GREENFIELD

Pray that success
will not come any faster
than you are able to endure it.

ELBERT HUBBARD

The successful people
are the ones who can think up things
for the rest of the world
to keep busy at.

DON MARQUIS

———

Every man who is high up
loves to think
that he has done it all himself;
and the wife smiles,
and lets it go at that.

JAMES M. BARRIE

———

What's money?
A man is a success
if he gets up in the morning
and gets to bed at night
and in between does what he wants to do.

BOB DYLAN

Every now and then,
when you're on the stage,
you hear the best sound a player can hear.
It's a sound you can't get
in movies or in television.
It is the sound of a wonderful,
deep silence that means you've hit them
where they live.

SHELLEY WINTERS

In the eyes of the people,
the general who wins a battle
has made no mistakes.

FRANÇOIS MARIE AROUET VOLTAIRE

Failure can be bought on easy terms;
success must be paid for
in advance.

CULLEN HIGHTOWER

TALENT

We must infer
that all things are produced
more plentifully and easily
and of a better quality
when one man does one thing
which is natural to him
and does it at the right time,
and leaves other things.

PLATO

The best investment
is in the tools of one's own trade.

BENJAMIN FRANKLIN

Latent abilities
are like clay.
It can be mud on shoes,
brick in a building
or a statue that will inspire
all who see it.
The clay is the same.
The result is dependent
on how it is used.

JAMES LINCOLN

———⋈———

No gain is so certain
as that which proceeds
from the economical use
of what you already have.

LATIN PROVERB

Better do a little well,
than a great deal badly.

SOCRATES

We judge ourselves
by what we feel capable of doing,
while others judge us
by what we have already done.

HENRY WADSWORTH LONGFELLOW

There is a natural aristocracy
among men.
The grounds of this
are virtue and talent.

THOMAS JEFFERSON

Pay no attention
to what the critics say;
there has never been a statue
erected to a critic.

JEAN SIBELIUS

The high prize of life,
the crowning glory of a man
is to be born with a bias
to some pursuit
which finds him
in employment and happiness—
whether it be to make baskets,
or broadswords, or canals,
or statues, or songs.

RALPH WALDO EMERSON

Genius is the gold
in the mine;
talent is the miner
that works and brings it out.

LADY MARGUERITE BLESSINGTON

What lies behind us
and what lies before us
are tiny matters
compared with what lies within us.

OLIVER WENDELL HOLMES

VISION

Genius is the quality
of the special spirit,
whether in poetry
or politics or science,
which raises a man
above a single locality or nation
to influence the people of the world.

CORNELIUS W. DE KIEWIET

The big ideas in this world
cannot survive
unless they come to life
in the individual citizen.
It is what each man does
in responding to his convictions
that provides the forward thrust
for any great movement.

NORMAN COUSINS

Imagination
lit every lamp in this country,
produced every article we use,
built every church,
made every discovery,
performed every act
of kindness and progress,
created more and better things
for more people.
It is the priceless ingredient
for a better day.

HENRY J. TAYLOR

Only he who can see the invisible
can do the impossible.

FRANK GAINES

The true test of a great man—
that, at least, which must secure his place
among the highest order of great men—
is, his having been in advance of his age.

HENRY BROUGHAM

Behind every advance
of the human race
is a germ of creation
growing in the mind
of some lone individual.
An individual whose dreams
waken him in the night
while others lie contentedly asleep.

CRAWFORD GREENEWALT

Far away in the sunshine
are my highest inspirations.
I may not reach them,
but I can look up
and see the beauty,
believe in them
and try to follow
where they lead.

LOUISA MAY ALCOTT

We think too small.
Like the frog
at the bottom of the well.
He thinks the sky
is only as big as the top of the well.
If he surfaced,
he would have
an entirely different view.

MAO TSE-TUNG

The important thing is this:
to be able at any moment
to sacrifice what we are
for what we could become.

CHARLES DU BOIS

I don't want people
who want to dance.
I want people
who have to dance.

GEORGE BALANCHINE

To play great music,
you must keep your eyes
on a distant star.

YEHUDI MENUHIN

If I have been able
to see farther than others,
it was because I stood
on the shoulders of giants.

ISAAC NEWTON

Don't part
with your illusions.
When they are gone
you may still exist,
but you have ceased to live.

MARK TWAIN

Let a man in a garret
but burn with enough intensity,
and he will set fire
to the world.

ANTOINE DE SAINT-EXUPERY

Whatever you do,
or dream you can do,
begin it.
Boldness has genius,
power and magic in it.

JOHANN WOLFGANG VON GOETHE

If you don't know
where you're going,
you'll end up somewhere else.

YOGI BERRA

WEALTH

Much learning
shows how little mortals know;
much wealth,
how little worldlings enjoy.

EDWARD YOUNG

Riches should be admitted
into our houses,
but not into our hearts;
we may take them
into our possession,
but not into our affections.

PIERRE CHARRON

That man is to be accounted poor,
of whatever rank he be,
and suffers the pains of poverty,
whose expenses
exceed his resources;
and no man is, properly speaking,
poor, but he.

WILLIAM PALEY

All the good things
of the world
are no further good to us
than as they are of use;
and of all we may heap up
we enjoy only as much
as we can use,
and no more.

DANIEL DEFOE

That which we acquire
with the most difficulty
we retain the longest;
as those who have earned a fortune
are usually more careful of it
than those who have inherited one.

CHARLES CALEB COLTON

That plenty should produce
either covetousness or prodigality
is a perversion of providence;
and yet the generality of men
are the worse for their riches.

WILLIAM PENN

Rich or poor,
it's good to have money.

SID LANCE

Money is the symbol of duty.
It is the sacrament
of having done for mankind
that which mankind wanted.

SAMUEL BUTLER

Everything you gather
is just one
that you can lose.

ROBERT HUNTER

There is a certain Buddhistic calm
that comes from having . . .
money in the bank.

TOM ROBBINS

Be not concerned
if thou findest thyself
in possession of unexpected wealth;
Allah will provide
an unexpected use for it.

JAMES J. ROCHE

—◆—

Men make counterfeit money;
in many more cases,
money makes counterfeit men.

SYDNEY J. HARRIS

—◆—

I am not rich.
I am a poor man with money,
which is not the same thing.

GABRIEL GARCIA-MARQUEZ

Who is rich?
He that is content.
Who is that?
Nobody.

BENJAMIN FRANKLIN

I am indeed rich,
since my income
is superior to my expense,
and my expense is equal
to my wishes.

EDWARD GIBBON

With money in your pocket,
you are wise
and you are handsome
and you sing well too.

YIDDISH PROVERB

To desire money
is much nobler
than to desire success.
Desiring money may mean
desiring to return to your country,
or marry the woman you love,
or ransom your father from brigands.
But desiring success
must mean that you take
an abstract pleasure
in the unbrotherly act
of distancing and disgracing
other men.

GILBERT K. CHESTERTON

Rule No. 1:
Never lose money.
Rule No. 2:
Never forget Rule No. 1.

WARREN BUFFETT

WISDOM

Be wise;
soar not too high to fall,
but stoop to rise.

PHILIP MASSINGER

The wise sometimes condescend
to accept of titles;
but none but a fool
would imagine them
of any real importance.
We ought to depend upon
intrinsic merit,
and not on the slender helps
of a title.

OLIVER GOLDSMITH

Knowledge always desires increase;
it is like fire,
which must first be kindled
by some external agent,
but which will afterwards
propagate itself.

SAMUEL JOHNSON

As soon as true thought
has entered our mind,
it gives a light
which makes us see a crowd
of other objects
which we have never perceived
before.

FRANÇOIS DE CHÂTEAUBRIAND

Ignorance is not bliss—
it is oblivion.

PHILIP WYLIE

❦

Keep the gold and keep the silver,
but give us wisdom.

ARAB PROVERB

❦

The art of life
is to know how to enjoy a little
and to endure much.

WILLIAM HAZLITT

❦

Sixty years ago I knew everything;
now I know nothing;
education is a progressive discovery
of our own ignorance.

WILL DURANT

'Tis not knowing much, but what is useful,
that makes a wise man.

THOMAS FULLER

All animals except man
know that the principal business of life
is to enjoy it.

SAMUEL BUTLER

Wisdom is divided into two parts:
(a) having a great deal to say,
and (b) not saying it.

ANONYMOUS

To know that which lies before us
in daily life
is the prime wisdom.

JOHN MILTON

The trick in life
is to decide what's your major aim—
to be rich, a golf champion,
world's best father, etc.
Once that's settled,
you can get on with the happy,
orderly process of achieving it.

STANLEY GOLDSTEIN

The wise know the value of riches,
but the rich do not know
the pleasures of wisdom.

HEBREW PROVERB

Perhaps one has to be very old
before one learns how to be amused
rather than shocked.

PEARL BUCK

WORK

The art of using moderate abilities to advantage
often brings greater results
than actual brilliance.

FRANÇOIS LA ROCHEFOUCAULD

The real price of everything
is the toil and trouble
of acquiring it.

ADAM SMITH

Failures are few
among people who have found
a work they like enough to do it well.
You invest money in your work;
invest love in it too.
Like your work.
Like the people with whom you work.
It pays well.

CLARENCE E. FLYNN

It is only the constant exertion and working
of our sensitive, intellectual, moral,
and physical machinery
that keeps us from rusting,
and so becoming useless.

CHARLES SIMMONS

What men want is not talent,
it is purpose;
in other words,
not the power to achieve,
but will to labor.
I believe that labor
judiciously and continuously applied
becomes genius.

EDWARD GEORGE BULWER-LYTTON

How do I work?
I grope.

ALBERT EINSTEIN

Fortune is ever seen
accompanying industry.

OLIVER GOLDSMITH

There is no boon in nature.
All the blessings we enjoy
are the fruits of labor,
toil, self-denial, and study.

W. G. SUMNER

This one makes a net;
This one stands and wishes.
Would you like to bet
which one gets the fishes?

CHINESE RHYME

To industry
nothing is impossible.

LATIN PROVERB

No fine work can be done
without concentration and self-sacrifice
and toil and doubt.

MAX BEERBOHM

Nothing comes easily.
My work smells of sweat.

ERIC HOFFER

A day's pay
for a day's work
is more than adequate
when both the work and the pay
are appreciated
as much as they are expected.

CULLEN HIGHTOWER

Find something you love to do
and you'll never have to work
a day in your life.

HARVEY MACKAY